A Song of Life

and Other Poems

by

Merrilee Bordeaux

ISBN 978-1-947514-07-2

Printed in the U.S.A

St. Clair Publications

P.O. Box 726

McMinnville, TN 77110-0726

http://stclairpublications.com

Cover design by Kent Grey-Hesselbein,

KGB Design Studio

Manchester, TN, USA

http://kghdesign.nvaazion.com/

Index

Author Bio

Merrilee Bordeaux is a native and resident of the small town of Franklin, North Carolina. A retired middle school teacher of language arts and social studies, she gains her inspiration from the beauty of God's Western North Carolina mountain area. The love, creativity, and compassion of her friends and family also help her find poetry in everyday events. Merrilee enjoys volunteering at her church and the community. She lives with two of her grandchildren and her beloved dog, Cocoa, who leads the cat clan.

Dedication

I dedicate this book of poetry to my granddaughter Lisa Walker, who has filled my retirement years with countless adventures and love.

Acknowledgement

I want to thank my old elementary and high school classmate, Stan St. Clair, for helping to make my dream come true by publishing this book of my poetry. Also, I want to express my deepest gratitude to the girls of the FHS class of '64 for their encouragement and friendship.

Fond Memories

A Song of Life

Running through gently falling raindrops,

Twirling with graceful artistic flair,

Tapping to a cheerful boogie beat,

Singing with melodious entrancing charm,

Sneaking behind the thickest tree,

Yelling, "Just try to find me, Mimi,"

Creating tall tales for neighborhood kids,

Twisting the ropes on the backyard swing

Then flying around the cloudless blue sky,

Tiptoeing up for a fun-filled tickle fest,

Floating in a pond of vivid imagination,

Stroking and cuddling her beloved cats,

Talking softly to the robins and squirrels,

Letting an inchworm crawl up an arm,

Laughing joyously with twinkling blue eyes,

Climbing from one tree limb to another,

Living life to the fullest lengths,

My vivacious granddaughter, Lisa,

Turning cartwheels on the soft velvety grass.

Editor's Choice Award, poetry.com

Poem published in "*Eternal Portraits*," International Library of Poetry

The Forgotten Soul

Huddling under a culvert near a lonely highway,

Stretching out, shivering, in a shell of an old Chevy,

Curling up awkwardly, stiffly on a city park bench,

I am the forgotten soul,

Winds ripping at torn, thin clothing,

Rains battering frozen limbs with heavy fists,

I am the forgotten soul,

Once I lived as a human with some dignity,

I worked, I laughed, I loved, I lived normally,

Now, I am the shame of the city, the suburbs, the small town,

I am the forgotten soul,

One smile, one jacket, one bowl of warm soup,

Please give me a little hope.

Editor's Choice Award, poetry.com

Published in "*Eternal Portraits*," International Library of Poetry

Listen to the Earth

The evergreens gently sweep the air,
The yellow daffodils sway to the beat,
Chirping robins, wrens, kittens' meows,
I feel the special rhythm in my bare feet.

The caterpillar crawls on the oak limb,
An inchworm investigates my thumb,
A song of praise, an evening hymn,
the bullfrog croaks deeply in praise.

A young kitten lazily bats a green stalk,
The black dog howls his neighborhood news,
The butterfly flits from peony to pansy,
The cows chew cud on the soft mews.

The colt frolics beside his watchful mom,
The children play joyful leapfrog in the yard,
The teeny chipmunk races across my loam,
Among the maples the squirrel pards dash.

The red dogwood holds a treasure dear,
Mother robin keeps a new family there,
The old cat naps in the warm morning sun
Mother Earth's work is nearly done.

Editor's Choice Award, poetry.com
Published in *"Sounds of Poetry,"*
International Library of Poetry

Earth's Music

As the morning dawns, earth's sounds are sweet,
squirrels chattering, "Let's play hide and seek,"
the birds happily do twitter and tweet,
"Let's fly down to the bubbling creek."

Hark, the silence of childhood antics,
No shrieks, no laughter, no cries at all,
Early morning misty veils do not panic
just quietly lift their ghostly eerie pall.

The sun tries warming her animal citizens,
While a lone hawk soars above the earth,
searching for a mouse or chipmunk denizen
to fill his aching stomach dearth.

Frolicking colts gallop with boundless mirth,
Rabbits hop jauntily, field mice scurry about,
Mud-rolled pigs eat slop adding to their girth
as eager spiders spin webs near the rain spout.

A plaintive plea, "Where's our worm, Mommy?"
the hungry baby robins chirp frantically,
A barn owl awakes somewhat grumpily,
"Whooo's noisily disturbing me?"

The mooing cows stroll into the lea,
The sheep kick up their lively heels,
A black snake slithers by a buzzing bee
wondering how to find a tasty meal.

The zooming, honking frustrated cars,
impatiently eager drivers missing the sounds
that everyday nature provides near and far,
Beauty, melody, soothing ambience abound

Some people don't even seem to care
that nature is alive with such variety,

A Song of Life and Other Poems

The neighing of a frightened mare,
A purring kitten crawling on a knee,

How could anyone possibly just ignore,
What loveliness Mother Earth has in store.

Editor's Choice Award, poetry.com
Published in *"Sounds of Poetry,"*
International Library of Poetry

Hope

While life is a fleeting, transient stage,
Accomplishments fill less than one page,
Benefit mankind with simple deeds,
To lost souls pay impassioned heed.

A few kind words, a gentle hug, a listening ear,
A warm meal, some good clothes, a ten or two,
Who knows how love reaches near or far,
Give each need one their just due.

Encouragement goes a long way to heal,
One's inner strife and turbulent woes,
Assist a homeless nomad to really peel
frustration, mottled skin, and filthy clothes.

Even though the outer part is streaked with mire,
distrust, fear, and confusion, reign within,
The soul you can still reach and inspire,
Hope is worth far more than silver or tin,

When approaching the serene heavenly heights,
Money or fame will not be the welcoming key,
Belief and faith in God will give insight
into what is really true about you and me.

July, 2004

Cloudy Comforts

Have you ever lain on soft grass in a lea,
Watched the clouds caress the mountains
encircling them and letting some escape
to peek out and take a short break,
What a breath-taking sight to watch,
Clouds lower than our highest hills,
Almost as if they had formed a special
ballerina's tutu and yet, they have
a special mystery to unfold,
Why hiding did they bow so low
from the restless, searching sky,
As I lie upon the velvety green carpet,
I began an adventure of imagination.
I can see the sky gently calling to the clouds
Come heavenward and float awhile
Dodging the rising sun and eagles' beaks
The floating wisps began to form
whoa, a pirate ship, a lamb, a rose thorn
A dragon rises and flies horizontally
listening to the busy, buzzing bees
Beautiful nature helps me feel serene,
Is there a God, some people say,
He is everywhere, all nature every day.

July, 2004

Seeds of Faith

Time is so short upon this earth,
Before you're ready God calls you home,
Work effortlessly with great mirth,
Help people repair their homes.

Know that your family depends on you
for comfort, hearth, food, and love
When family troubles erupt near you.
You are the peace-making dove

Your children will always try
to emulate your thoughts and deeds,
Act courageously before you die,
Your actions are your mightiest seeds.

Your neighbors see you try to do right,
You work hard most nights and days
to try to aid all in your sight,
to make your life not stray.

The way you live your life each day
is the prayer to God who reigns over all,
Strive to believe and live His way,
or you will have little witness at all.

October, 2004

The Wrath of Ivan

One fateful September eve, a violent storm
slammed furiously on a Macon mountainside,
Perry's Creek was just a little ole trickle
that became an uproarious violent fist,
A fist which knocked on top of the mountain,
dealt a blow to everything, daring to be in its way,
The whole mountainside was swept away,
like a gigantic bulldozer had destroyed all,
Nothing left could ever be the same,
The roaring water caused all a terrified chill,
The entire side of the mountain took an awful spill,
The torrential rain forever changed Perry's Creek,
But the tale of distressing eve is hardly done,
The bravery and loving inspiration of all the residents,
The fire and rescue workers so daring and bold,
The doctor who slid under an unstable house
just to help an injured woman out,
Not many will hear all the tales of our brave ones,
who fought the wind, water, other obstacles that night,
For all the unsung heroes not only in Perry's Creek,
but everywhere in our besieged country with loving aid,
You gave your all to wounded people in body and soul,
The wrath of the storm took many things, yet hope remained.

December, 2004

Anticipation

My grandchild's face pressed into the window,
Hope building cautiously and then running
like a frisky gangly colt in the meadow,
Icy fairies dancing in a silent ballet,
Then angry, furious hordes rushing downward
filling the air, hurtling in every direction,
suspense mounting in her dreams and hopes,
Is this the special day, the anticipated one,
When finally she can ride her plastic steed
flying down the mountainside like a cougar,
Participate in a round contest of flight,
Her packed missile against her friend's
skilled aim and speed,
Suddenly her arms take wings, her feet hope gleefully,
The snow is really, sticking to the frozen raceway.

February, 2005

Editor's Choice Award, poetry.com
Published in *"Sounds of Poetry,"*
International Library of Poetry

Memories of FHS

Forty years ago came the timid, bold, and in-between,
Searching for acceptance, love, knowledge and more,
Sports, clubs, Laurel Leaf, The Mountain Echo 'twen
English, algebra, science, and Mrs. Campbell's store.

Our teachers crammed theories and facts in our minds,
They inspired and stretched our creative thought,
Exacting standards were there to constantly remind
Great expectation for us they wrought.

When we goofed up they used special tact
to help and encourage us and get us back,
How very fortunate we were to have them
to harvest the best in us back then.

Dribbling, shooting for the basketball hoop.
Tackling, swiftly passing the football,
Marching, tuning with a fancy swoop,
Taking pictures, memories for us all.

Without a single, fleeting doubt,
Our experiences at good ole FHS,
Molded characters and changed lives,
All of us still try to be our best.

July, 2004

Mr. D's ABCs

Aim for high goals and ambitions,
Bring your pencil and paper to class,
Concentrate on English, not boys,
Deliver your research paper on time,
Energize your active fertile brains,
Fill your paper with fertile thoughts,
Give your honest effort every day,
Have confidence in your writing ability,
Identify with caring peers,
Mention kind remarks to a friend,
Notice what your neighbor is doing well,
Open your heart to others,
Read daily to feed a lifetime habit,
Sit in class with a little decorum,
Talk when you can contribute to a discussion,
Use only number 2 pencils or black ink pens,
Value your classmates, friends, teachers,
Wait for your ability to mature,
Xerox very sparingly,
Yell not when you lose your cool,
Zealously pursue your goals.

June, 2004

The Fog

Morning wore a gray misty cloak,
It covered my beloved mountain lair,
I saw no deer grazing warily in the meadow,
No fat- cheeked chipmunks with nuts in their mouths,
Even the absence of squirrels chattering the news,
Morning had painted a surreal eerie scene,
Traces of fall to be found nowhere,
No reddish blushes of autumn love,
No golden leaves floating in the wind,
Where, oh where, is my gorgeous morn,
Only silence fills my strange day,
Morning seems to have gone away,
I miss my black cat sitting on the porch rail,
The scarecrow swaying in the breeze,
When, oh when, will I be able to see
Morning, please change your mourning cloak,
I want you dressed in your autumn best.

November, 2005

The Airborne Frog

As my granddaughter was happily swimming in the pool,
floating, stroking beneath the soft watery blue,
She surfaced for some cool refreshing air,
What to her curious blue eyes should appear
but a tiny baby plastic frog drifting near,
Yet when touched, proved to her dismay
to be quite real and wiggly that day,
Now she doesn't mind an inchworm crawling on her arm,
or a lightning bug jetting off from her hand,
But an amphibian who pees, poops, where he swims,
Was no creature she could stand,
A gallant champion swam forth to aid her plight,
"I'll get the varmint for you, miss,"
At a mighty sling the frog did fly,
down to the muddy pond nearby,
Quickly grinning, the stranger dove out of sight,
saving her from a gruesome fright.

July, 2004

Sir Dragon

The silver dragon opened his clear-blue eyes,
Stretched his shining violet scaled wings,
Rose on his strong turquoise legs and feet,
His diamond toenails capturing the sun's rays,
Perking up his chartreuse ears he grinned,
As a puff of happiness wafted from his mouth,
The melodious song floated to him in the air,
The tunes his beloved maiden sang had no peer,
So beautiful, sweet, and gentle was she
Lady Melissa had won the dragon's heart and loyalty,
As the dragon flapped his massive wings soaring through the air,
he watched as his lady did brush her long blond hair,
Melissa rested on a boulder by the bubbling creek,
As she talked softly to the birds, deer, foxes nearby,
she sighed and gazed rather wistfully around,
Then the giant dragon did gently come to land
to see if he could give his lady a helping hand,
As a bluebird flew by her glowing pink cheeks,
Sir Dragon gently patted her soft lily arms,
The blue sky and rising sun warmed them.

July, 2005

Late Summer's Morn

Whispering pines moaning softly,
Maple leaves waving gently,
Robins speaking urgent news,
Three cats soaking the summer rays,
Caterpillars inching toward green lunch,
Ants marching in rapid columns,
Orange berries dancing in the breeze,
Children jumping on the trampoline,
Dishwashers cleaning plates and pots,
Brooms sweeping the storm debris,
Distant tires swishing on wet roads ,
Lawnmowers mowing soft grass,
Grapevines filling with vitamin C,
Dogs barking the latest gossip,
Cows meandering, munching in the lea,
Fish frolicking in the calm creek,
Teenagers washing their wheeled steeds,
Washing machines cleaning the week's merriment,
Mops ridding houses of dirt and grime,
Mothers helping children become squeaky clean,
A late summer's morn.

August 2004

Why

My brute charges toward me like the most fearsome bull,
Yet I am not a famous matador, just a terrified child,
Cowering, dreading what always comes next,
Trying to find safety and comfort,
A fist grabs my hair and pulls me up and up,
What pain - my legs, a kicked soccer ball
to my beast, my face, a punching bag,
Tears stream down my frightened face,
Sobbing, wondering what I did wrong,
Blood runs down my face, gagging me,
Barely gasping, I whisper, "Pleeease stop."
I wish I could call for help from someone,
but I caused my monster to get mad, didn't I,
I hope I can live to the age of eight,
I have some time to try to breathe,
'cause he's passed out.
Time to clean away the blood, but I
can't clean away the fear and hurt,
I just want to ask him, why,
Why, Daddy, do I make you so angry,
Why, Daddy, do you want to hit me,
Daddy, do you want me to die?

April, 2005

No More Peanut Butter

I was sittin' round the stump of an old oak tree
watchin' the goings on of the birds and the bees,
When what to my curious eyes should appear,
but a vivacious active little black bear,
The little sprite ambled right on over
to see if I had any special treats
like blueberries, strawberries, or the like
even walnuts, blackberries, might hit the spot,
When he smelled the peanut butter and jelly,
he raised up on his hind legs on the dot
with one swift swoop his mouth did grab
my only sandwich, and he did really chew,
Alas no more had I, I knew well
one little morsel fills no baby bear
So he commenced to search everywhere
in my pocket, my knapsack, my trousers, too
He wasn't as gentle as I wished he would be,
I was afraid I'd end up black and blue,
When looking up for higher help,
I spotted my salvation, with a nasty twist,
There on that ole nearby tree
was the biggest wasp nest my eyes had ever seed,
With one swift toss, I might knock it down
but that would sure enough mean
angry bees would hurtle to the ground,
They'd dive for bear cub and me,
Oh me, what a fix I was in,
Save myself to get stung again and again,
or be tossed around for a peanut butter snack,
So I decided to give the nest a whack,
sure enuf them mad wasps did dive bomb the bear,
but there was enough to get me everywhere,
So I did roll into a ball, twirling down the hillside,
As fast as I could roll along the trail,
I started a strange kind of avalanche
of leaves, twigs, nuts, rocks, and such,

Faster and faster I went finally
slamming into a yucky water-filled ditch,
As I struggled to find my legs and arms
Chawing peanut butter had lost its charm,
I crawled and limped my way home,
jest couldn't stand to touch my dome,
The moral of this tale, if there is one at all
Is when going for a hike in the wilderness,
Be sure to take no food,
especially peanut butter and jelly.

July 2004

A Song of Life and Other Poems

A Song of Life and Other Poems

Family

A Song of Life and Other Poems

A Special Traveler

God once sent a special traveler, Bonnie, to Earth
to meet, fall in love with, and mate with Phillip,
Now He has taken her back home to heaven
And we are left to remember our Bonnie,
Her hands were always busy with myriad things,
Her special skills with crochet and hand work,
Turning the pages of some of her favorite books,
Planting, pruning, growing her roses and such,
Calling her mother in-law, Velma, for
flower growing advice and other stuff,
Then celebrating their scented blooms with her,
Emailing her interested relatives and friends,
Keeping up with the latest news from pen pals,
Her handwritten letters were such a special treat,
Phillip was her soul mate, her support to the end,
A quiet boy who grew to be an extraordinary husband,
Bonnie depended on him in so many ways,
He was her rock, her chauffeur, her beloved mainstay,
Together they created three children, Mark, Kristen, and Kae,
Children are special gifts for couples to share,
Even though God has called her home,
Bonnie will always live in our hearts, our pictures,
Our memories will be even more treasured,
Bonnie is at rest now, no aches or pains,
We pause, sharing how she touched each of our lives.

November, 2005

My Mom

A graceful eagle riding the wafts of air,
A slick dolphin caressing the ocean blue,
A squirrel racing across the maple trees,
A soft kitten cuddling near Lisa and me,
None of these sights is quite so dear
as my Mom when she is coming near,
When Buzz and I were growing up,
Straight and tall we had to stand,
Friends just loved to come to our house
to eat potato salad, fried chicken, and lemon pie,
It was so good we ate until we had to stop,
She enjoyed eating with friends, and
I remember the picnics now and then,
Her sweet melodies charmed the house,
Her sense of humor had no peer,
That is why today she still brings cheer,
At First Baptist she gave so much
Outreach, choir director, and such,
She was an encourager with a kind word to say,
She would brighten each and every day,
When we were older, Gas, RAs, band, Boy and Girl Scouts
into everything that interested us, she lent a hand,
Mom read to us and so did our Dad,
Learning was always encouraged around our house,
Although Buzz was always smarter than me,
I read everywhere, anytime, you see,
While Buzz and Dad were enjoying fishing,
I would be curled up reading a book,
and today reading is my hobby,
Mom gave us a special legacy,
Love your family and your friends,
Be active, don't just sit around,
Find out what is needed to improve our town,
That is why as I volunteer somewhere each day,
I can hear Mom saying, "That's the way!"
I love my Mom, her courage and good sense,

A Song of Life and Other Poems

On this her eighty-fourth birthday we give tribute
Mom, we are glad out of all the moms in the world,
You are ours, and we just want to say, "We love you!"

The Hunk

There is a man of some special renown,
Noted for his flirtin' ways and joyous smiles,
Velma enjoys his sexy physique
and looks forward to more than a kiss on the cheek,
After being in his company for just a while,
We all know he makes our lives worthwhile,
At first the mountains he wished to vanish
replaced by rolling surf and ocean sands,
but soon windy breezes and scenic waterfalls
worked their magical spell on even our Willie,
Growing a garden was his new thing to do,
Lisa loves his tomatoes and cucumbers, too,
Fishing is his favorite sport, 'sides hugging Velma close,
Willie likes the women, both grown and small,
But he loves his Velma the best of all
He likes to talk and socialize,
Enjoying friends and eating good food,
You haven't eaten sumptuous food at all
until one of his fish fries, summer or fall,
On this his ninety-first birthday, we all cheer
for Willie, Velma's hunk, who has become so dear.

August 24, 2004

Our Living Angel

Some people believe in their guardian angels
that seem to keep trouble from heading their way,
But we have a muse and inspiration here on earth
Our living angel, Velma, teaches by example, each day,
She is an example of humble love and faithful strength,
Embracing the love of the almighty in a faithful way,

Velma shares and gives a smile that fills the heart,
Her smile dazzles and is brighter than the sun,
Her hugs warm those who need their mood to start
changing to a more cheerful feeling and then a grin,

Velma is a compassionate, humble woman without peer,
She speaks words of wisdom we would do well to heed,
Stranger or friend is better by having her near,
Her gentle nature, hugs, and kisses nourish our soul,
To live our lives just like her should be our daily deed,

A master gardener extraordinaire Velma has become,
Growing everything from A to Z, asparagus to zucchini,
Within her touch all fauna feel welcome,
Her beautiful roses fill all of us with envy,
Velma works hard, laughs often, cries some,
Loving family and friends her strength may be,

But positive encouragement and support she lives,
Each family member, friend, owes their success
to the nourishment her friendship gives,
She motivates each of us to try to live our best,
Her stylish dress, her fancy hats, her home décor,
Goodness, there isn't room for more,

Velma, you are truly the wings beneath our feet,
On this, your birthday, we do celebrate,
Our hero, our living angel, our mentor, our friend.

May, 2005

The True Southern Lady

Hours spent bent down picking out the weeds from her
priceless treasures,
Beautifying Franklin around the clock tower, the roadways,
everywhere she went asking for donations for flowers and tree,
never being turned down,
'Cause Merle was always busy beautifying all Franklin town,
She didn't stop with flowers and trees,
she arranged flowers for any need,
Karaoke on Friday night was graced with a single rose
on each Gazebo table,
Not only beautiful music and song from Larry, her son,
but breathtaking flowers to thrill your soul,
This tells but part of her intriguing story, though,
Every time you talked to her,
You felt like she hung on every word,
Her gift of listening to others
is a legacy we should all adopt,
While a teacher she did challenge and inspire,
She went more than that extra mile,
Former students still lovingly, proudly recall,
The award they won for being first over all
in arranging flowers, as one principal recalls,
"We learned far more than our ABC's and arithmetic",
She took the curriculum to such soaring heights,
And then added on so students were enthralled,
Life became a daily learning thrill,
Books became an adventure to read and share,
Creative glitter bulletin boards had none to compare,
But this is still not all there is to tell,
As a hostess she was without peer,
A house so clean you could eat off the floor,
Sumptuous veggies, meats, and goodies galore,
Yet those individual fried apple pies were the tastiest
The house was a haven for Larry and Richards' friends,
Everything she does, Merle does with loving grace,
She is a real southern lady with caring charm always in place,

Prelo like to kid her and say outrageous things for fun,
but you better never say anything negative about his Merle
All in all, she is only one of a few persons
who everyone would like to emulate,
Merle, the model of intelligence and compassion,
So today on your ninetieth birthday
You need to know how many lives you have touched,
and how much your loving ways have meant to us.

September, 2004

The Gentle Soul

Ray Vanhook

The gentle soul never met a stranger;
Ray would walk along his road,
Stopping here and there to chat a bit,
Giving other folks such a special lift.

Ray grew his vegetables to eat and give away,
He helped every soul who came his way,
You just talked to him sometimes,
Your spirits felt better all the while.

He liked to carve his wooden gifts,
Clocks, bowls, and wondrous stuff,
To this day I still treasure and admire
my bowl he carved with such care.

He loved his family with such strength,
Children always wanted to climb on his lap,
Ray, my best friend's father, a mentor to us all,
Living the Golden Rule was his life's call.

Even though he had a gentle love for life,
His special love was always Louise, his wife,
Fifty-eight years they spent together side by side,
Greatly inspiring strangers friends alike,

Now God has called him home to paradise,
Though we will miss him greatly each day,
He left us a special legacy, be active in our
community, love each other, and pray.

Ray helped his community, his church, his friends,
He battled cancer with grace to the end,
Family and friends now have a daily dare
to live our lives with loving care.

Ray, everyone who knew you was really blessed
by your Christian soul, your unique humbleness,
You wanted no special praise for what you did,
all of us are better for knowing your good Samaritan ways.

www.ingramcontent.com/pod-product-compliance
Lightning Source LLC
Chambersburg PA
CBHW021921040426
42448CB00007B/858